GRAPHIC LIBRARY™

GRAPHIC SCIENCE

THE DYNAMIC WORLD OF
CHEMICAL REACTIONS

WITH

MAX AXIOM™

SUPER SCIENTIST

by Agnieszka Biskup | illustrated by Cynthia Martin and Barbara Schulz

Consultant:
Leslie Flynn, PhD
Science Education, Chemistry
University of Minnesota
Twin Cities Campus

CAPSTONE PRESS
a capstone imprint

Graphic Library is published by Capstone Press,
1710 Roe Crest Drive, North Mankato, Minnesota 56003.
www.mycapstone.com

Library of Congress Cataloging-in-Publication Data is available on the Library of Congress website.

ISBN: 978-1-5435-5872-2 (library binding)
ISBN: 978-1-5435-6005-3 (paperback)
ISBN: 978-1-5435-5882-1 (eBook PDF)

Summary: In graphic novel format, follows the adventures of Max Axiom
as he explains the science behind chemical reactions.

Designer
Alison Thiele

Colorist
Matt Webb

Production Specialist
Laura Manthe

Cover Artists
Tod G. Smith and
Krista Ward

Media Researchers
Wanda Winch and
Jo Miller

Editor
Christopher Harbo

Photo Credits
Capstone Studio: Karon Dubke, 29, back cover; Shutterstock: Natalia
Klenova (inset) 6, Peter Hermes Furian (inset), 13

Printed in the United States   5725

TABLE OF CONTENTS

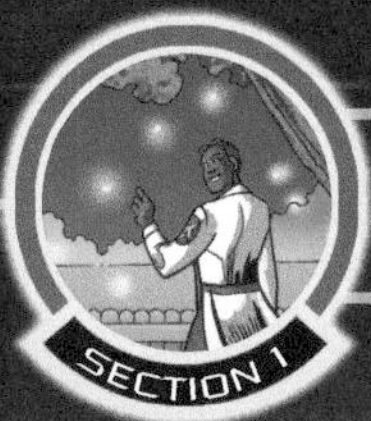
SECTION 1

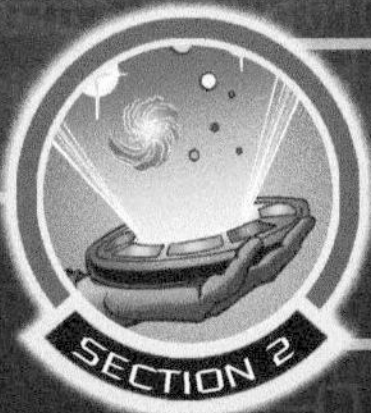
SECTION 2

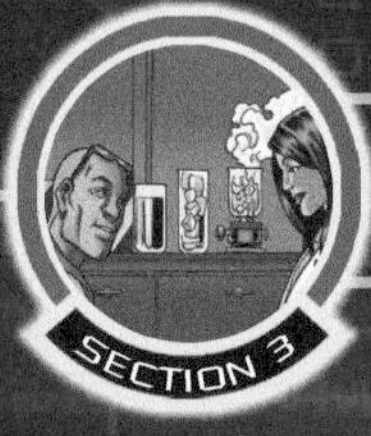
SECTION 3

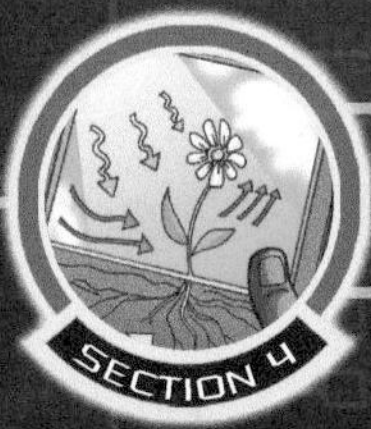
SECTION 4

Super scientist Max Axiom begins thinking about chemical reactions while enjoying an evening bonfire.
Nothing's better than a fire on a cool night!
Burning is one of the most important chemical changes, or reactions, around.
Chemical reactions happen when one substance is changed into a new substance.
In a fire, wood changes into ash and smoke.

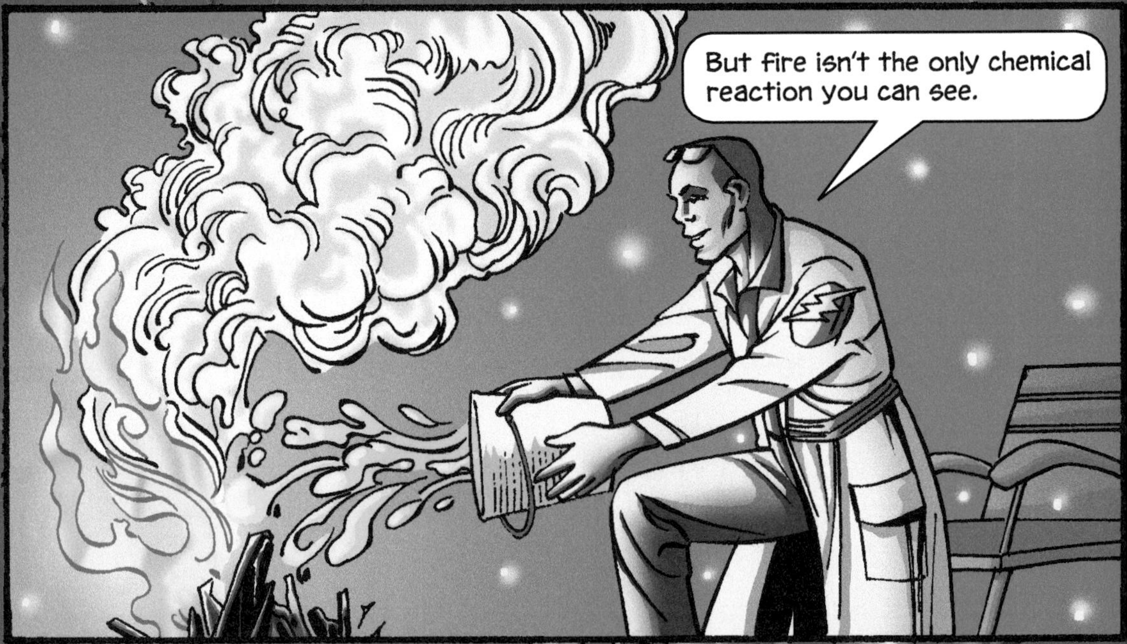
But fire isn't the only chemical reaction you can see.

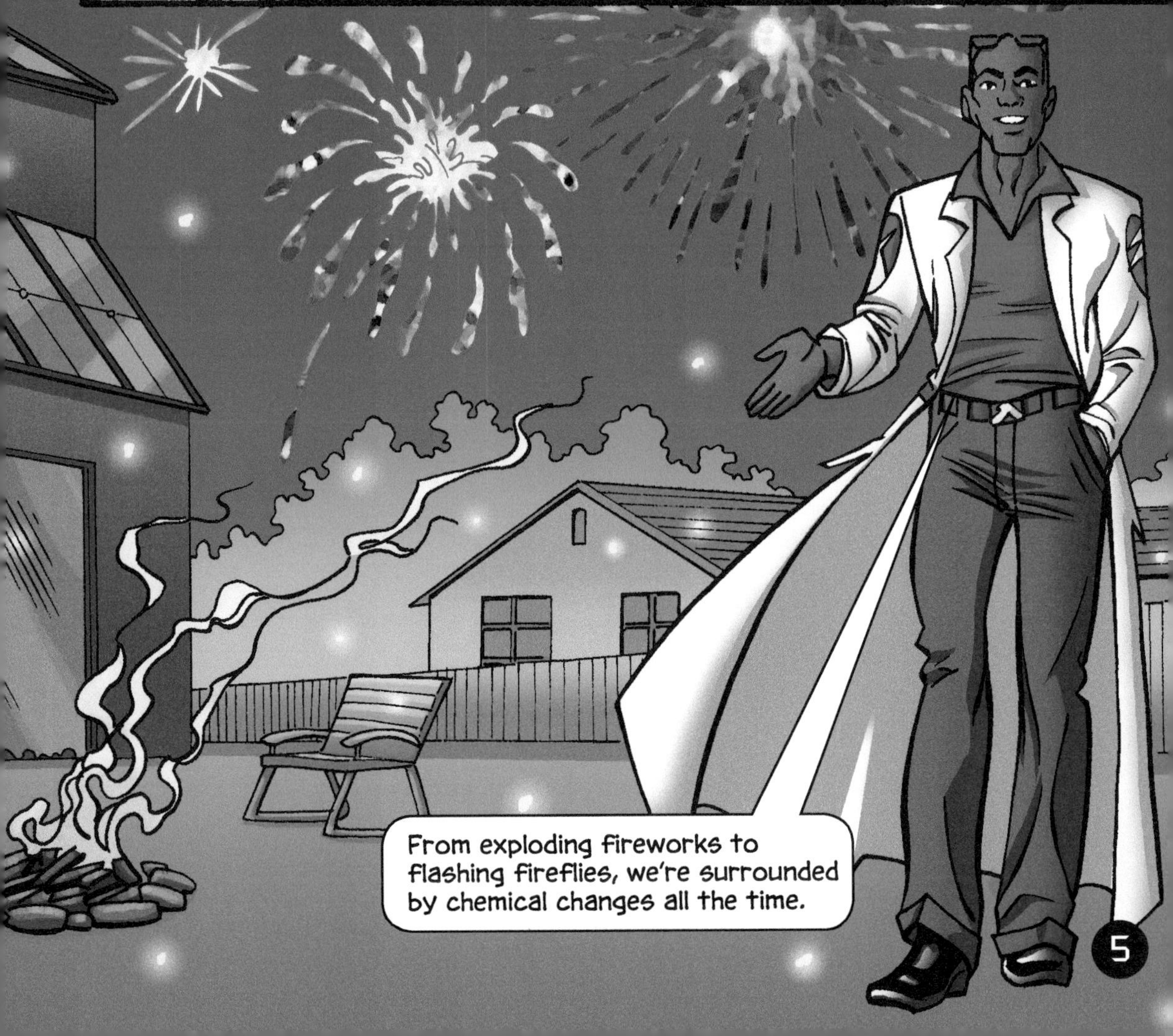
From exploding fireworks to flashing fireflies, we're surrounded by chemical changes all the time.

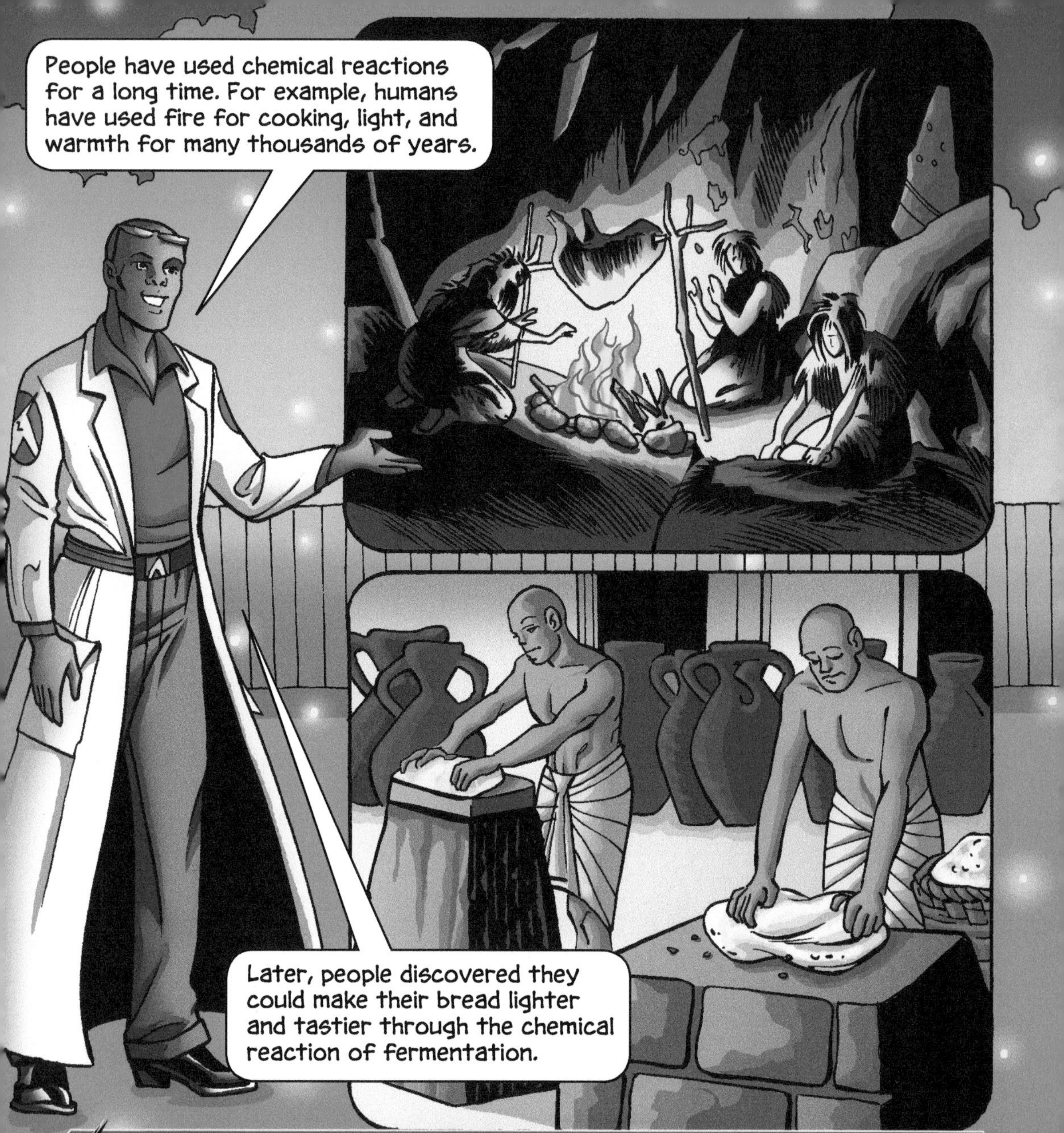
People have used chemical reactions for a long time. For example, humans have used fire for cooking, light, and warmth for many thousands of years.
Later, people discovered they could make their bread lighter and tastier through the chemical reaction of fermentation.

FERMENTATION

ACCESS GRANTED: MAX AXIOM

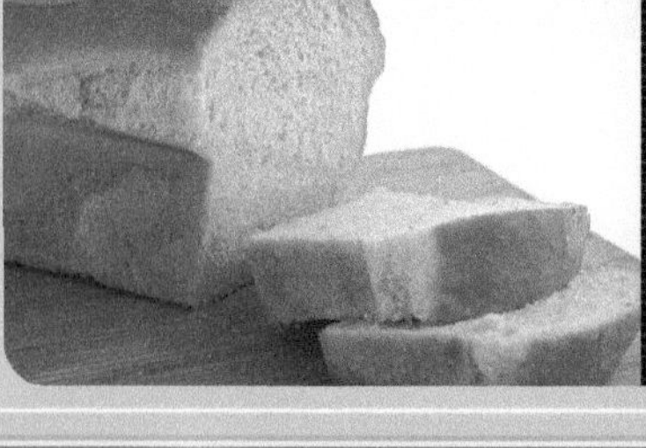

Fermentation can be used to produce various foods and beverages. It results when bacteria or yeast digest simple sugars. This digestion process gives off carbon dioxide gas and ethyl alcohol. It is the release of carbon dioxide gas that makes bread dough rise.

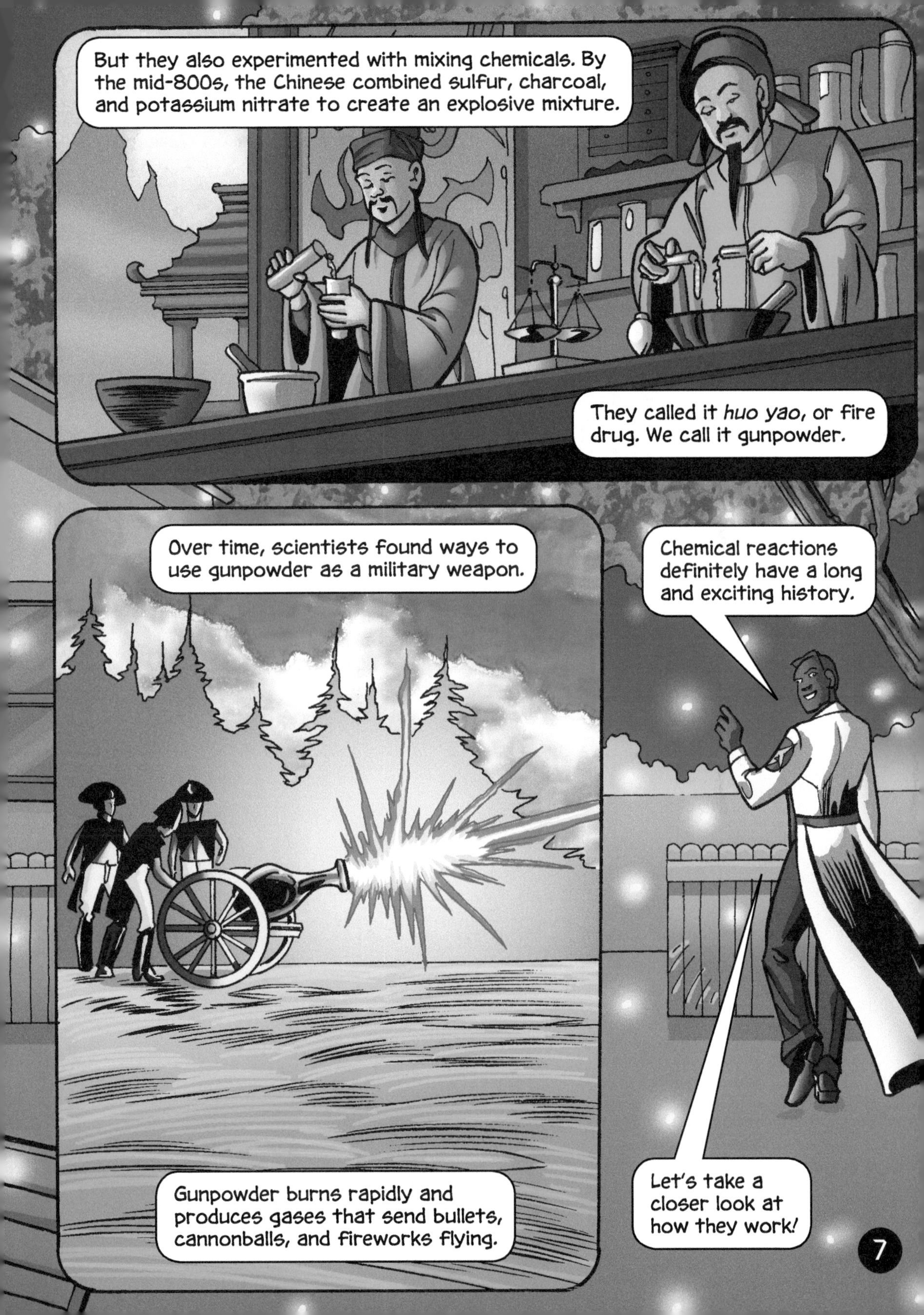
But they also experimented with mixing chemicals. By the mid-800s, the Chinese combined sulfur, charcoal, and potassium nitrate to create an explosive mixture.
They called it *huo yao*, or fire drug. We call it gunpowder.
Over time, scientists found ways to use gunpowder as a military weapon.
Gunpowder burns rapidly and produces gases that send bullets, cannonballs, and fireworks flying.
Chemical reactions definitely have a long and exciting history.
Let's take a closer look at how they work!

SECTION 2 MATTER, ATOMS, AND MOLECULES

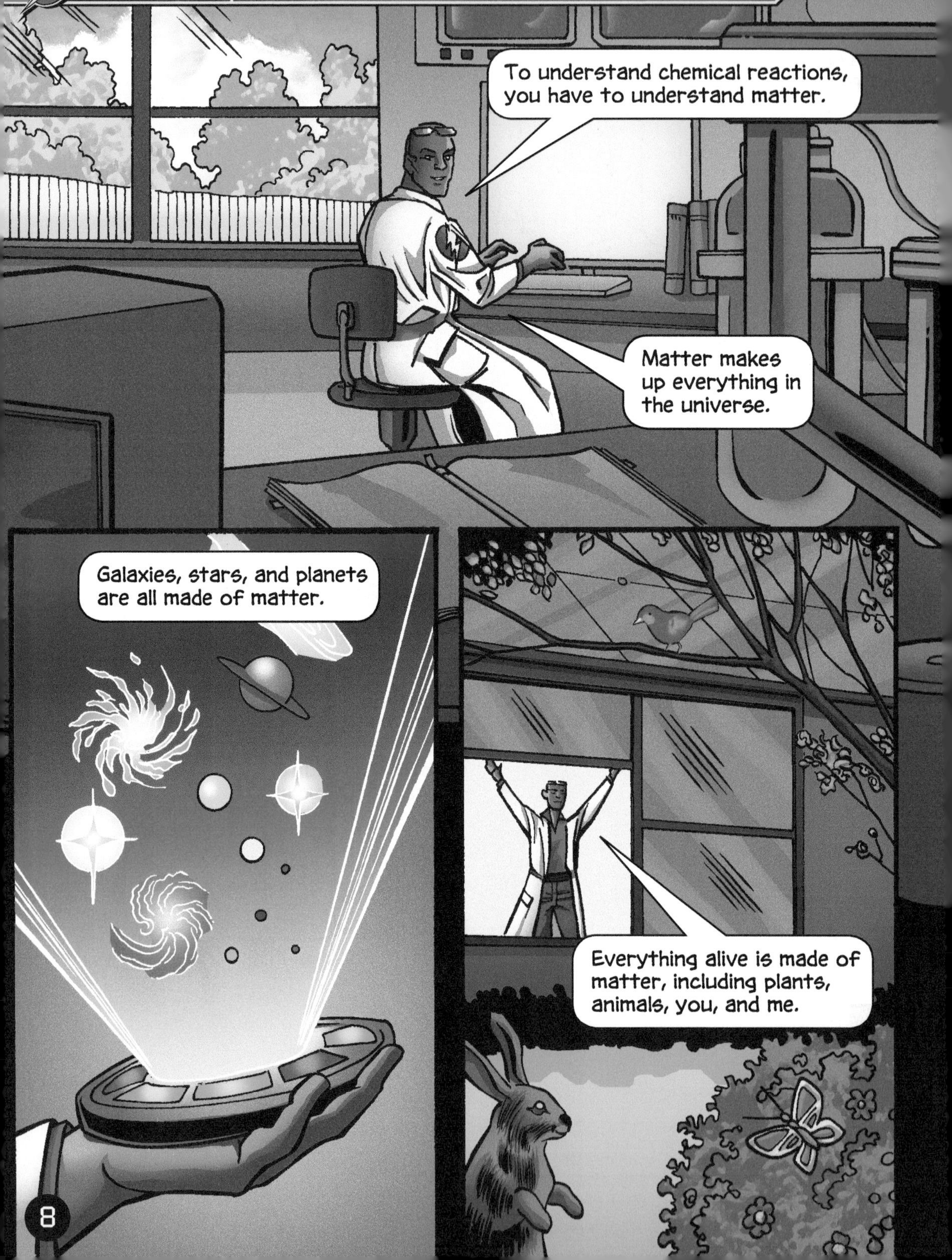
To understand chemical reactions, you have to understand matter.
Matter makes up everything in the universe.
Galaxies, stars, and planets are all made of matter.
Everything alive is made of matter, including plants, animals, you, and me.

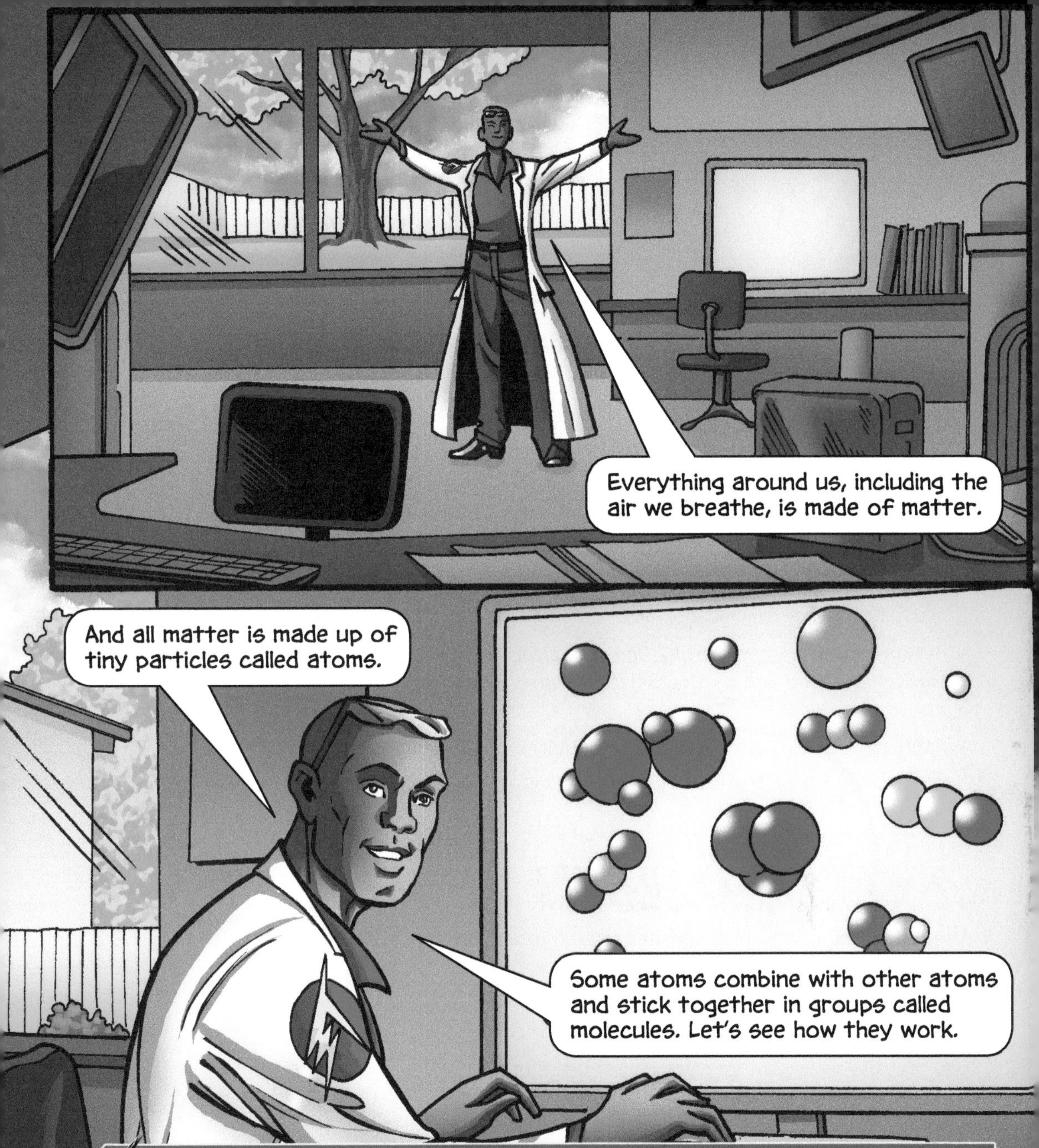
Everything around us, including the air we breathe, is made of matter.
And all matter is made up of tiny particles called atoms.
Some atoms combine with other atoms and stick together in groups called molecules. Let's see how they work.

INSIDE THE ATOM

ACCESS GRANTED: MAX AXIOM

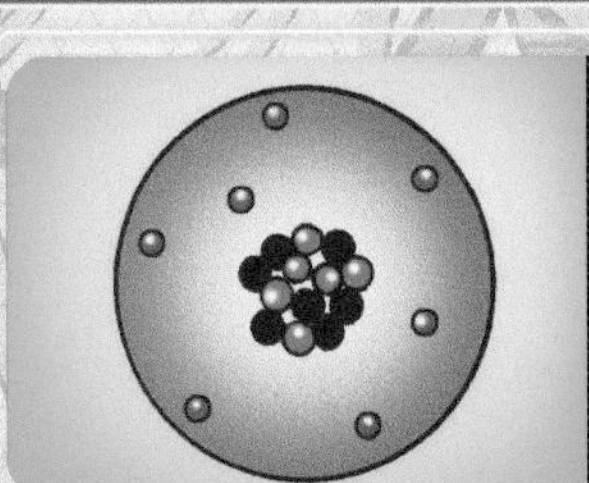

Atoms can be broken down into even smaller particles called neutrons, protons, and electrons. Protons and neutrons stick together at the center of the atom, called the nucleus. Electrons whiz superfast all around the nucleus.

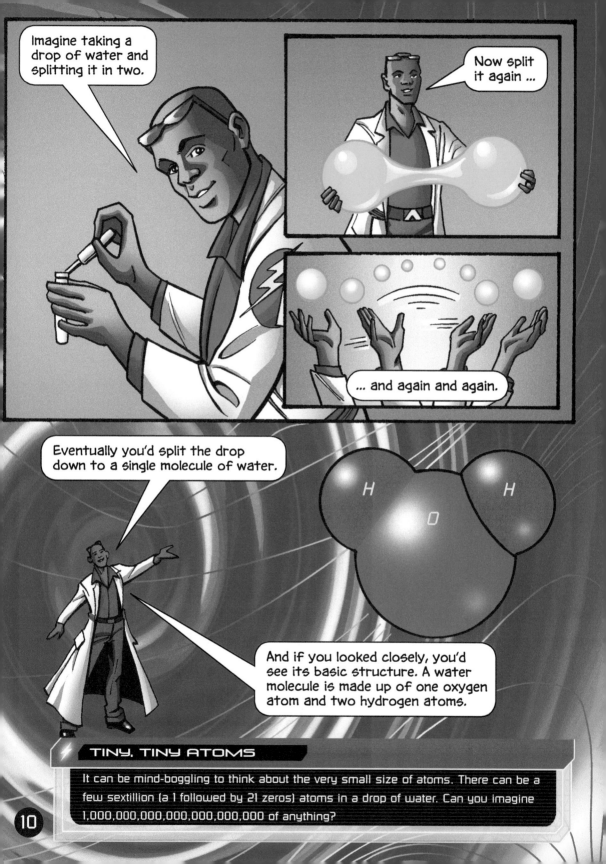

Imagine taking a drop of water and splitting it in two.

Now split it again ...

... and again and again.

Eventually you'd split the drop down to a single molecule of water.

H

O

H

And if you looked closely, you'd see its basic structure. A water molecule is made up of one oxygen atom and two hydrogen atoms.

TINY, TINY ATOMS

It can be mind-boggling to think about the very small size of atoms. There can be a few sextillion (a 1 followed by 21 zeros) atoms in a drop of water. Can you imagine 1,000,000,000,000,000,000,000 of anything?

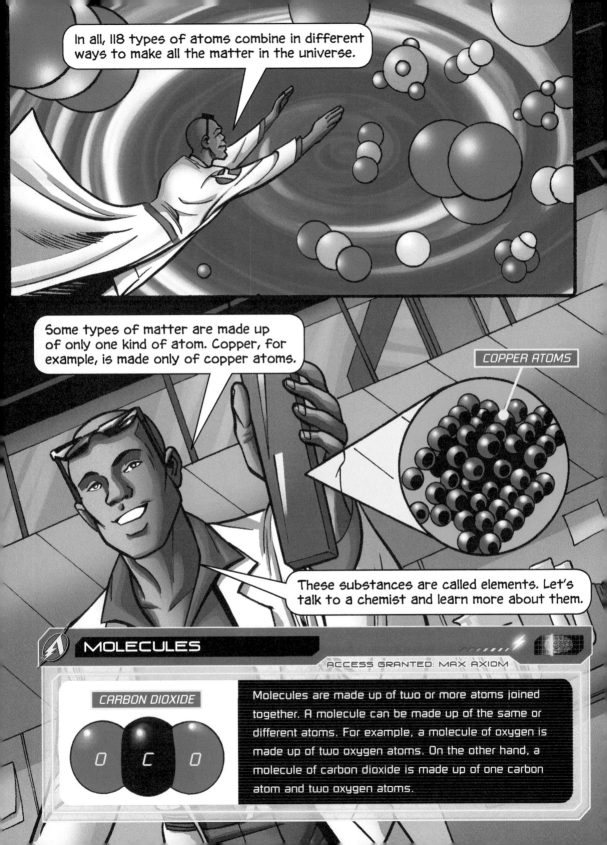

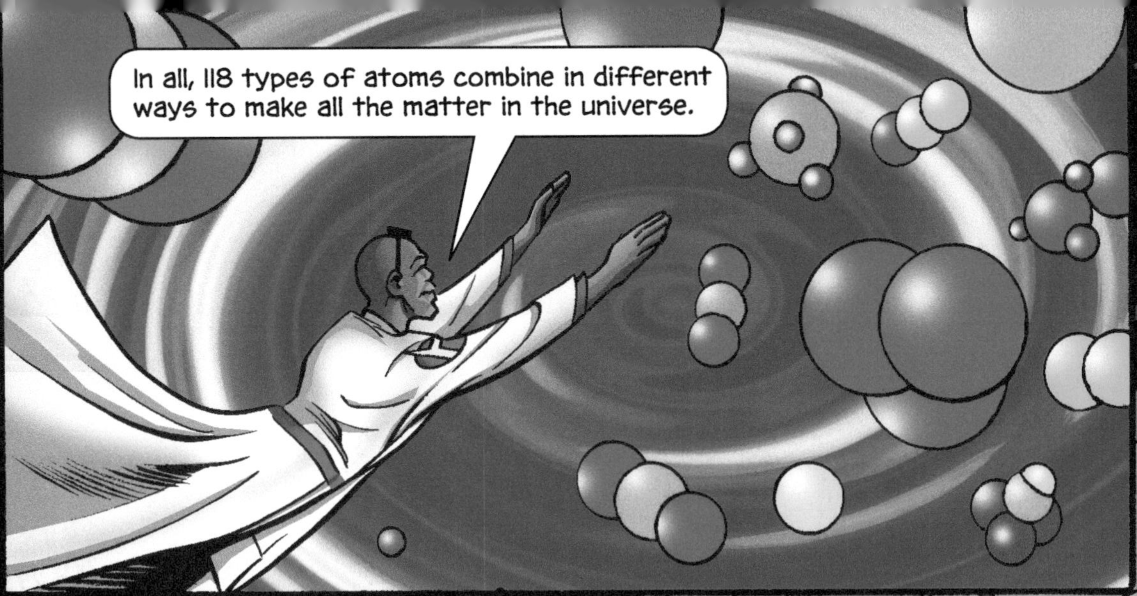
In all, 118 types of atoms combine in different ways to make all the matter in the universe.

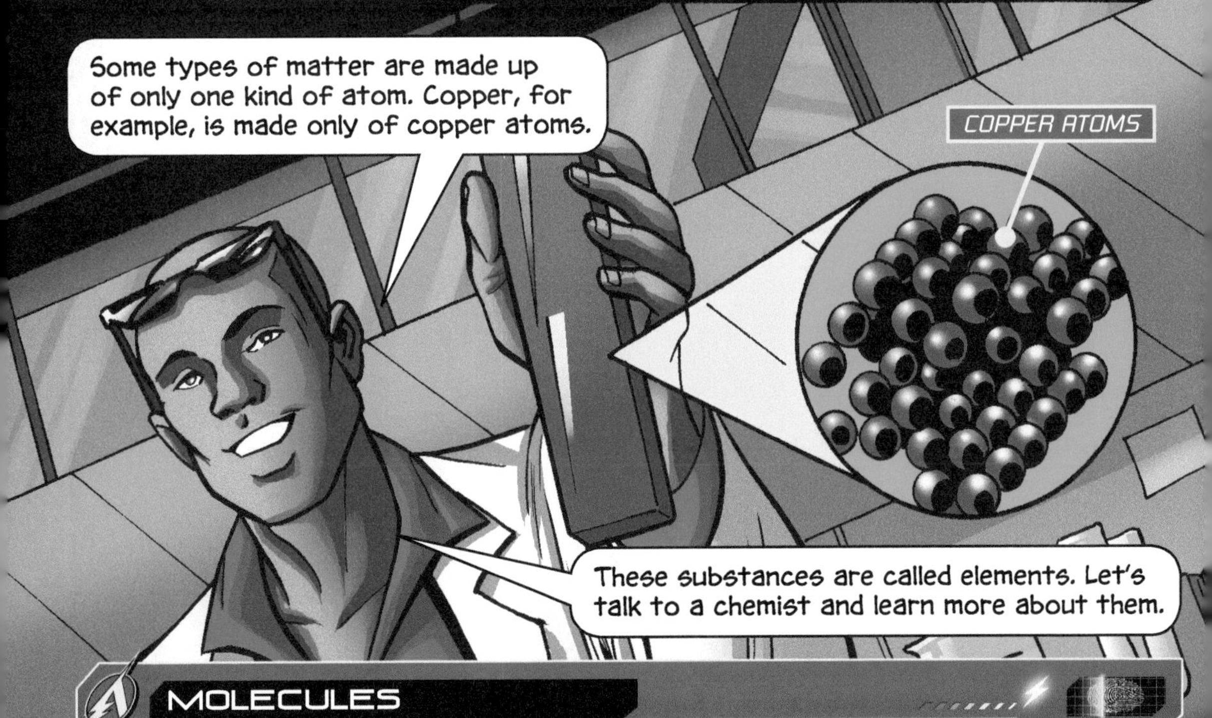
Some types of matter are made up of only one kind of atom. Copper, for example, is made only of copper atoms.
COPPER ATOMS
These substances are called elements. Let's talk to a chemist and learn more about them.

MOLECULES

ACCESS GRANTED: MAX AXIOM

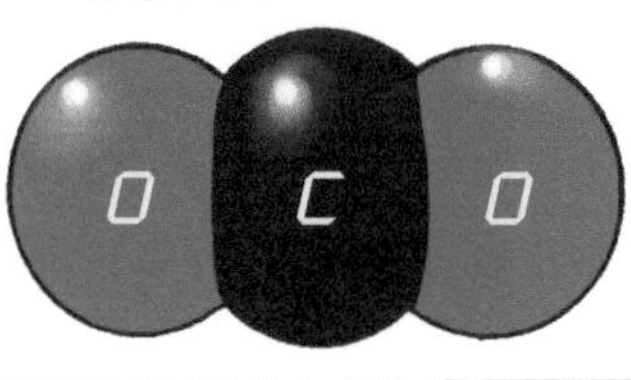
CARBON DIOXIDE
O
C
O

Molecules are made up of two or more atoms joined together. A molecule can be made up of the same or different atoms. For example, a molecule of oxygen is made up of two oxygen atoms. On the other hand, a molecule of carbon dioxide is made up of one carbon atom and two oxygen atoms.

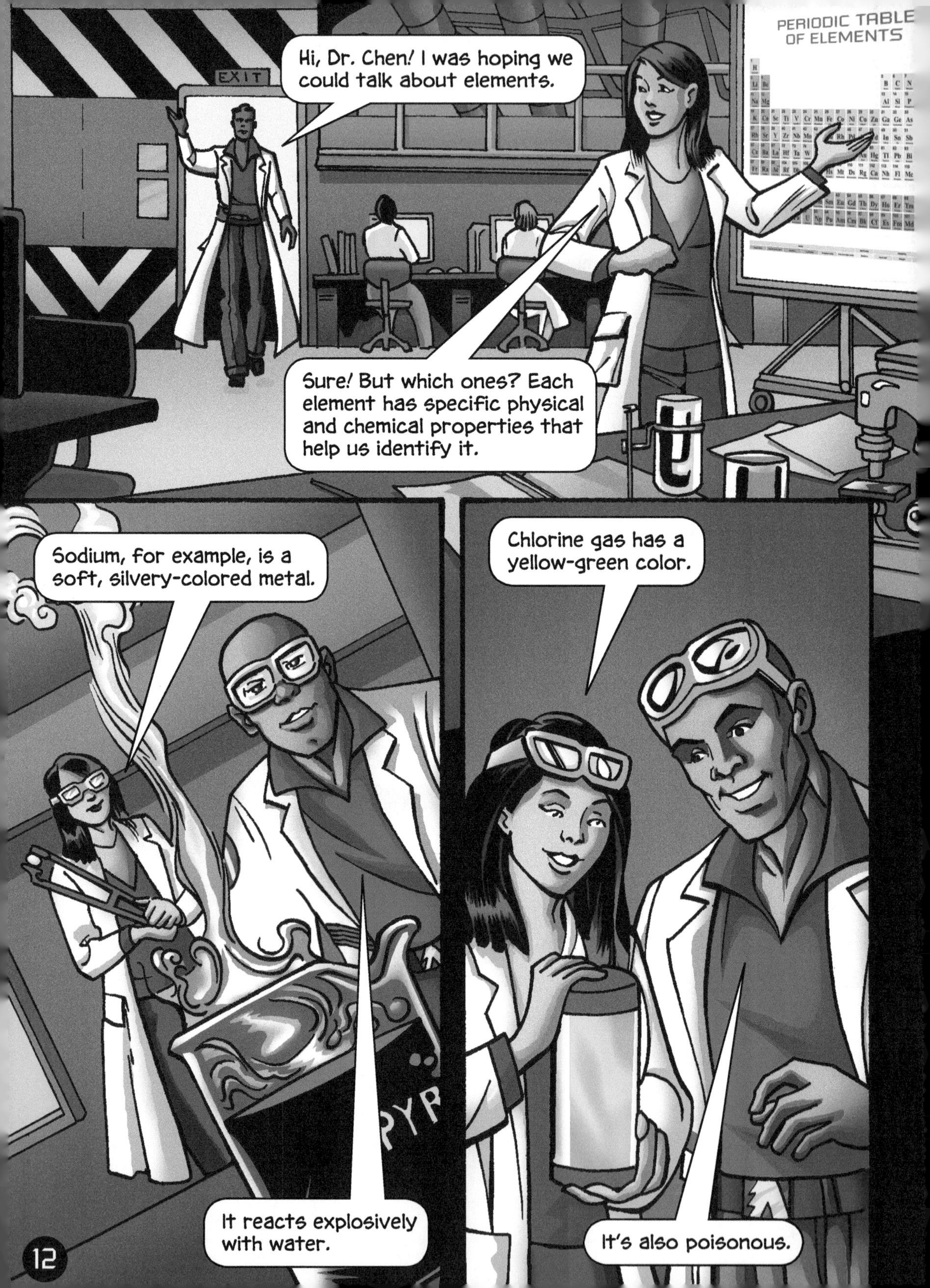
EXIT
PERIODIC TABLE OF ELEMENTS
Hi, Dr. Chen! I was hoping we could talk about elements.
Sure! But which ones? Each element has specific physical and chemical properties that help us identify it.
Sodium, for example, is a soft, silvery-colored metal.
It reacts explosively with water.
Chlorine gas has a yellow-green color.
It's also poisonous.

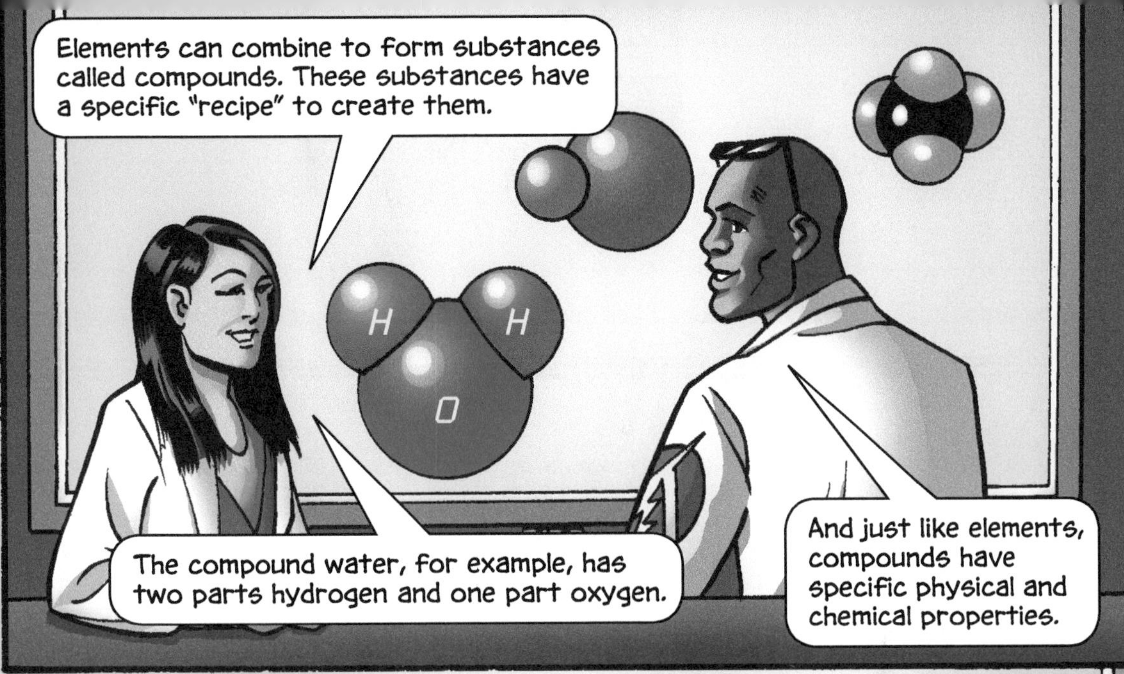
Elements can combine to form substances called compounds. These substances have a specific "recipe" to create them.
H
H
O
The compound water, for example, has two parts hydrogen and one part oxygen.
And just like elements, compounds have specific physical and chemical properties.

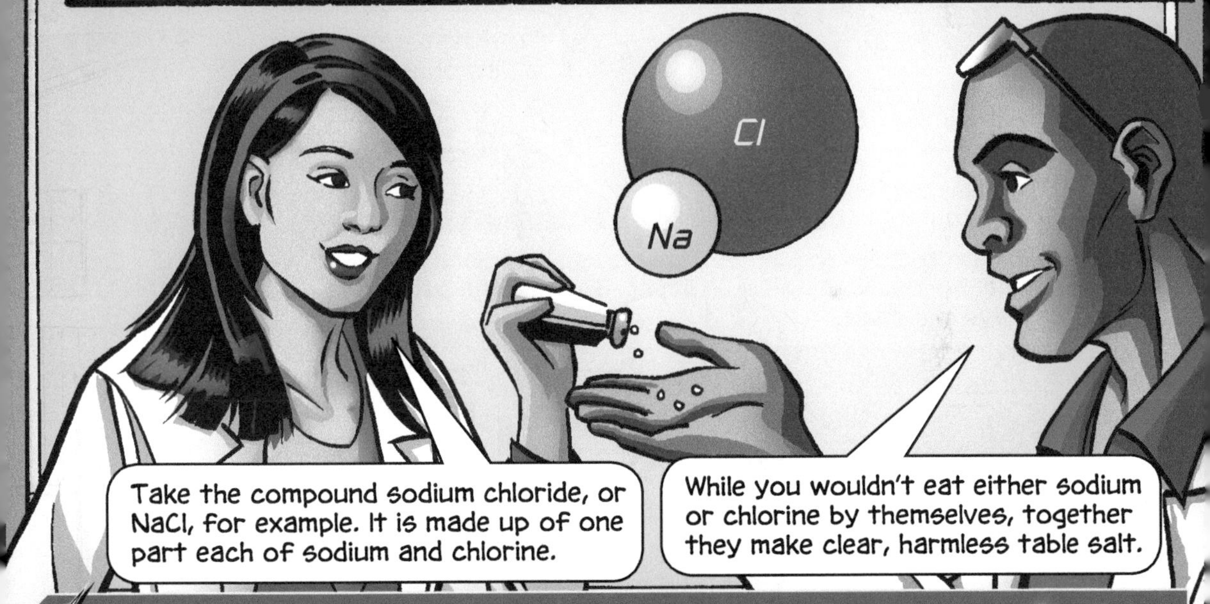
Cl
Na
Take the compound sodium chloride, or NaCl, for example. It is made up of one part each of sodium and chlorine.
While you wouldn't eat either sodium or chlorine by themselves, together they make clear, harmless table salt.

PERIODIC TABLE OF ELEMENTS

ACCESS GRANTED: MAX AXIOM

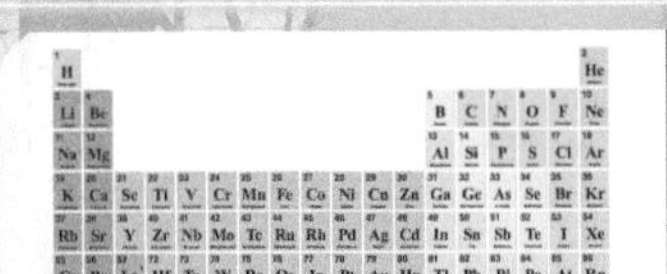

The periodic table of elements lists all the elements. It shows the physical characteristics of each element and helps scientists predict how elements will react when mixed together. On the periodic table, each element has its own symbol. Hydrogen's symbol is H, oxygen's is O, carbon's is C, chlorine's is Cl, and sodium's is Na.

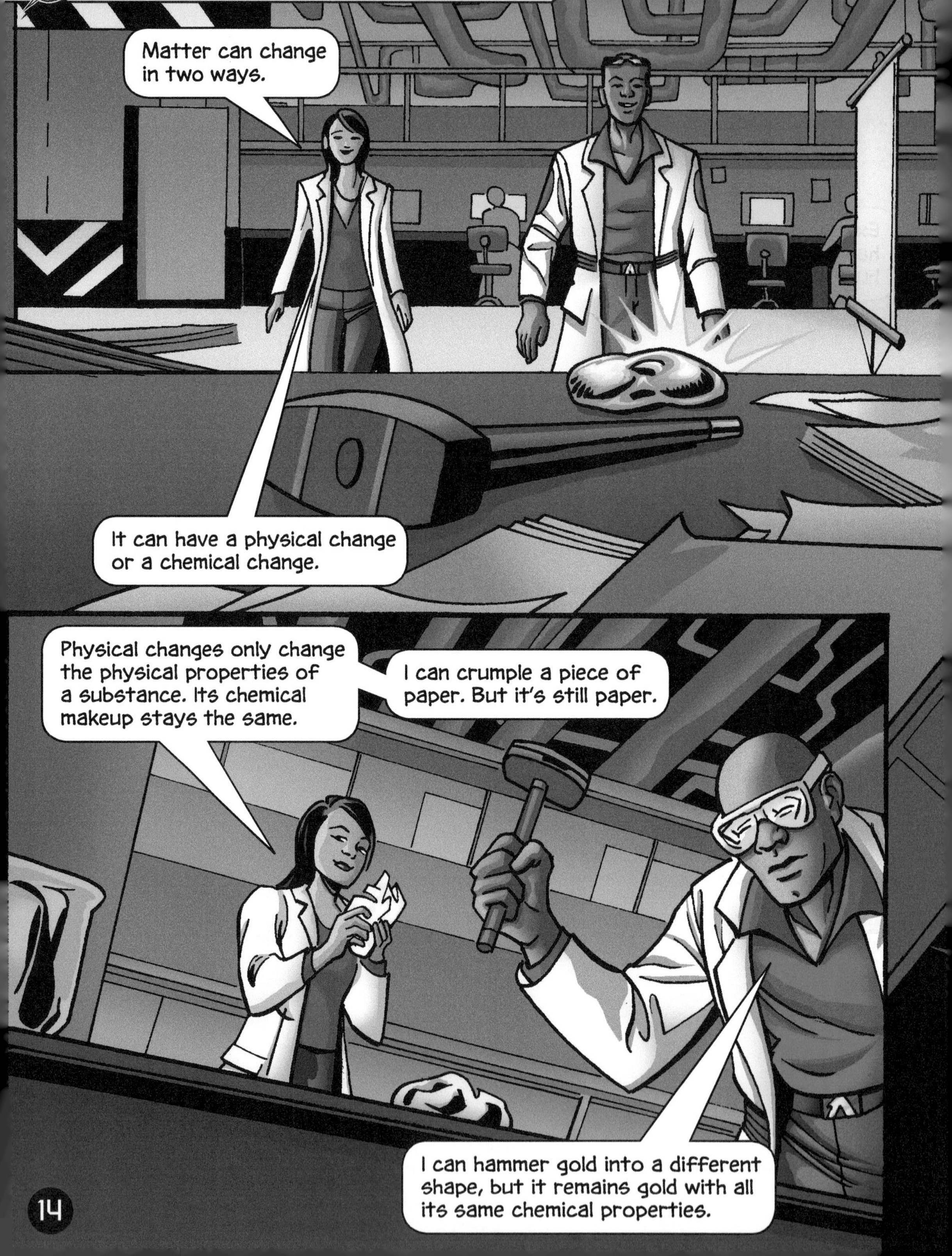
Matter can change in two ways.
It can have a physical change or a chemical change.
Physical changes only change the physical properties of a substance. Its chemical makeup stays the same.
I can crumple a piece of paper. But it's still paper.
I can hammer gold into a different shape, but it remains gold with all its same chemical properties.

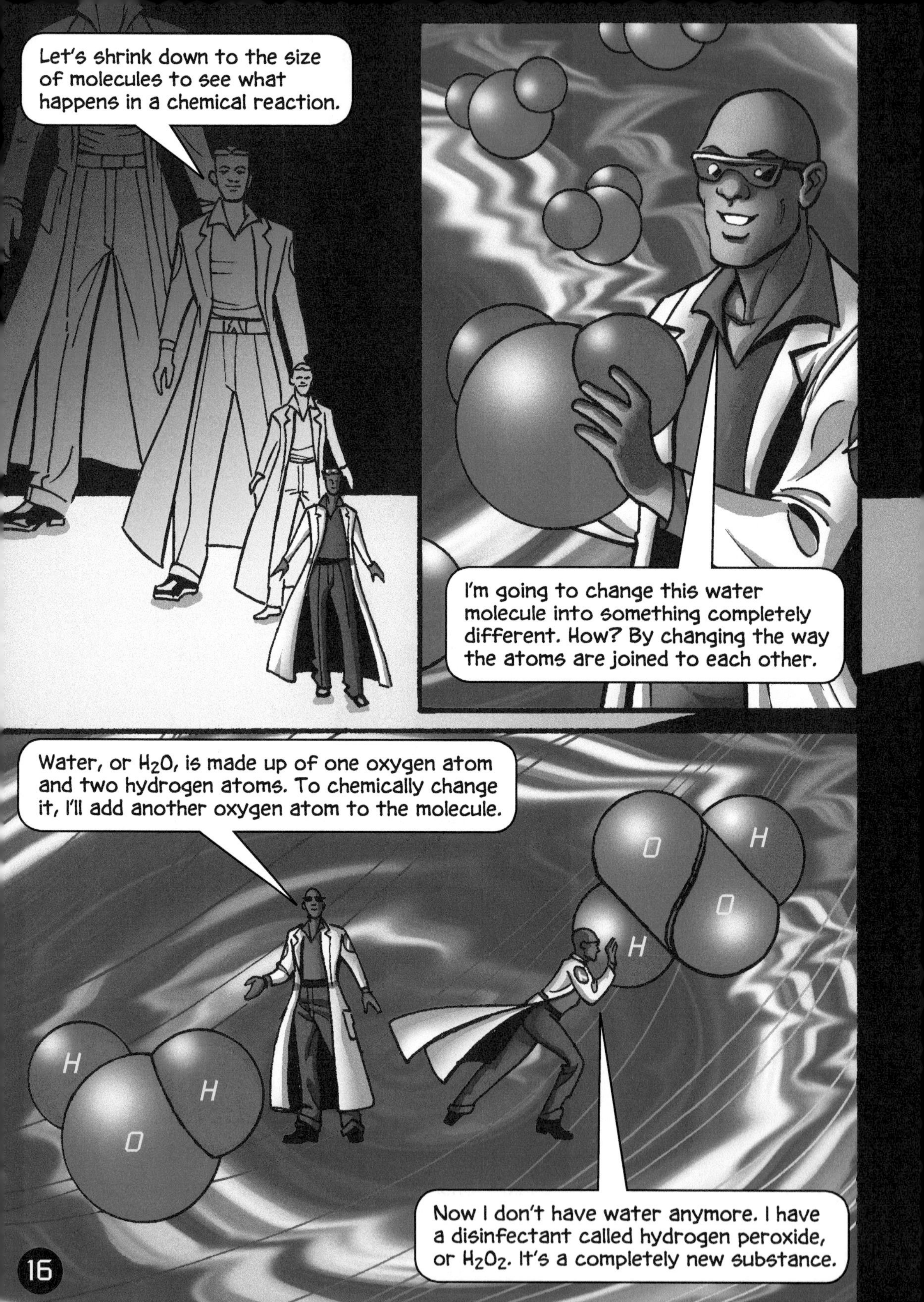
Let's shrink down to the size of molecules to see what happens in a chemical reaction.
I'm going to change this water molecule into something completely different. How? By changing the way the atoms are joined to each other.
Water, or H_2O, is made up of one oxygen atom and two hydrogen atoms. To chemically change it, I'll add another oxygen atom to the molecule.
O
H
O
H
H
H
O
Now I don't have water anymore. I have a disinfectant called hydrogen peroxide, or H_2O_2. It's a completely new substance.

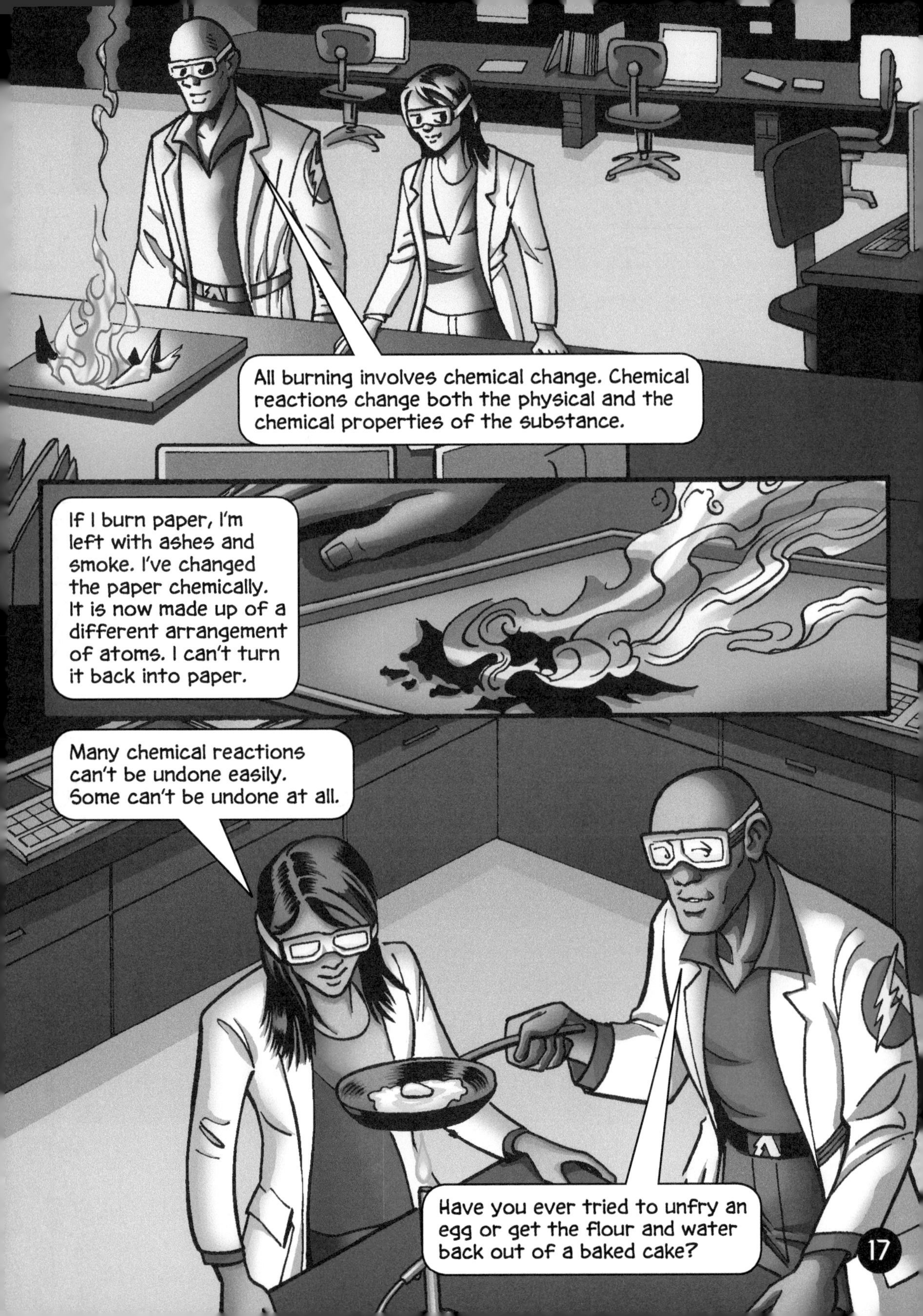
All burning involves chemical change. Chemical reactions change both the physical and the chemical properties of the substance.
If I burn paper, I'm left with ashes and smoke. I've changed the paper chemically. It is now made up of a different arrangement of atoms. I can't turn it back into paper.
Many chemical reactions can't be undone easily. Some can't be undone at all.
Have you ever tried to unfry an egg or get the flour and water back out of a baked cake?

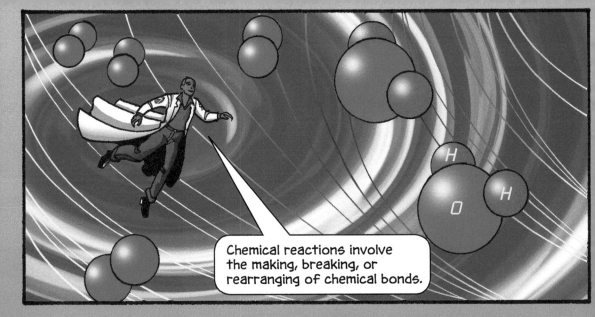

Chemical reactions involve the making, breaking, or rearranging of chemical bonds.

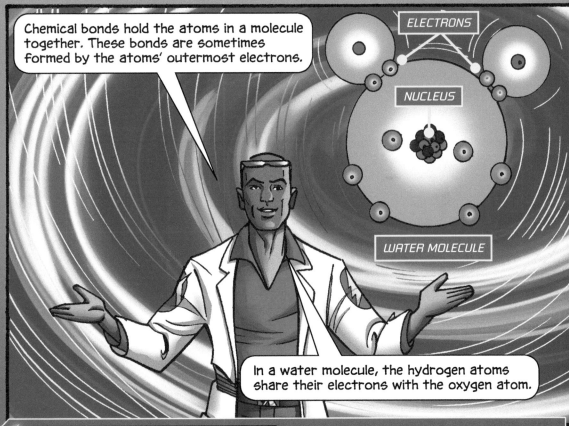

Chemical bonds hold the atoms in a molecule together. These bonds are sometimes formed by the atoms' outermost electrons.

ELECTRONS

NUCLEUS

WATER MOLECULE

In a water molecule, the hydrogen atoms share their electrons with the oxygen atom.

REACTANTS AND PRODUCTS

In a chemical reaction, the substances that undergo a chemical change are called the reactants. The substances that result from the change are called the products.

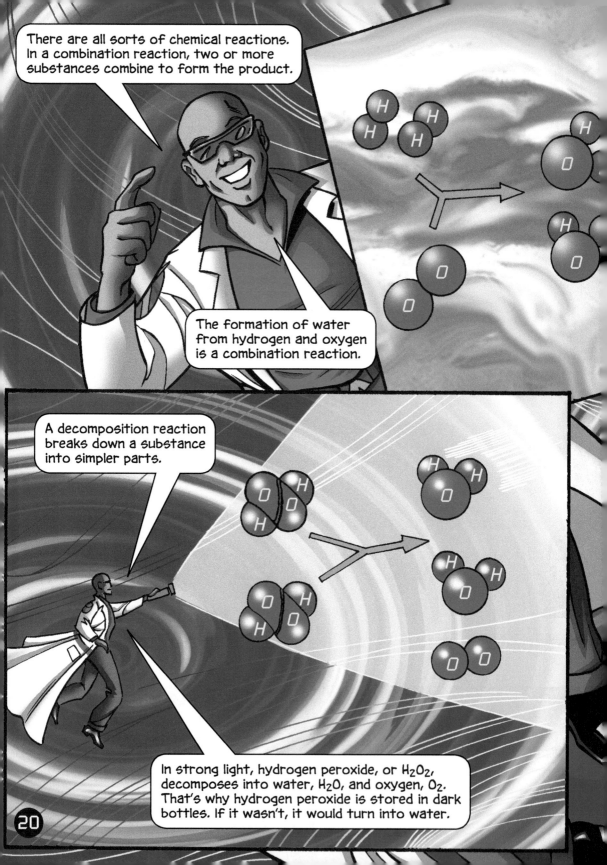

There are all sorts of chemical reactions. In a combination reaction, two or more substances combine to form the product.

The formation of water from hydrogen and oxygen is a combination reaction.

A decomposition reaction breaks down a substance into simpler parts.

In strong light, hydrogen peroxide, or H_2O_2, decomposes into water, H_2O, and oxygen, O_2. That's why hydrogen peroxide is stored in dark bottles. If it wasn't, it would turn into water.

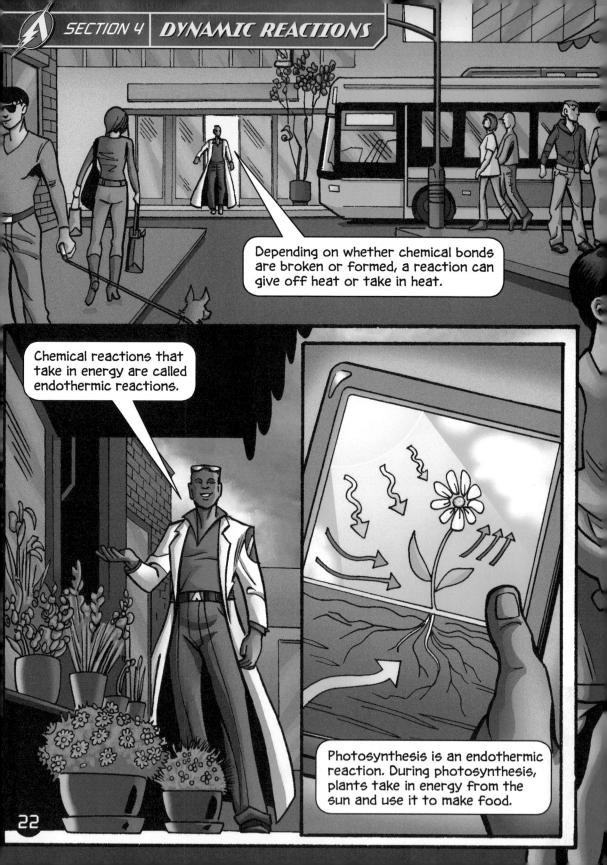

Depending on whether chemical bonds are broken or formed, a reaction can give off heat or take in heat.

Chemical reactions that take in energy are called endothermic reactions.

Photosynthesis is an endothermic reaction. During photosynthesis, plants take in energy from the sun and use it to make food.

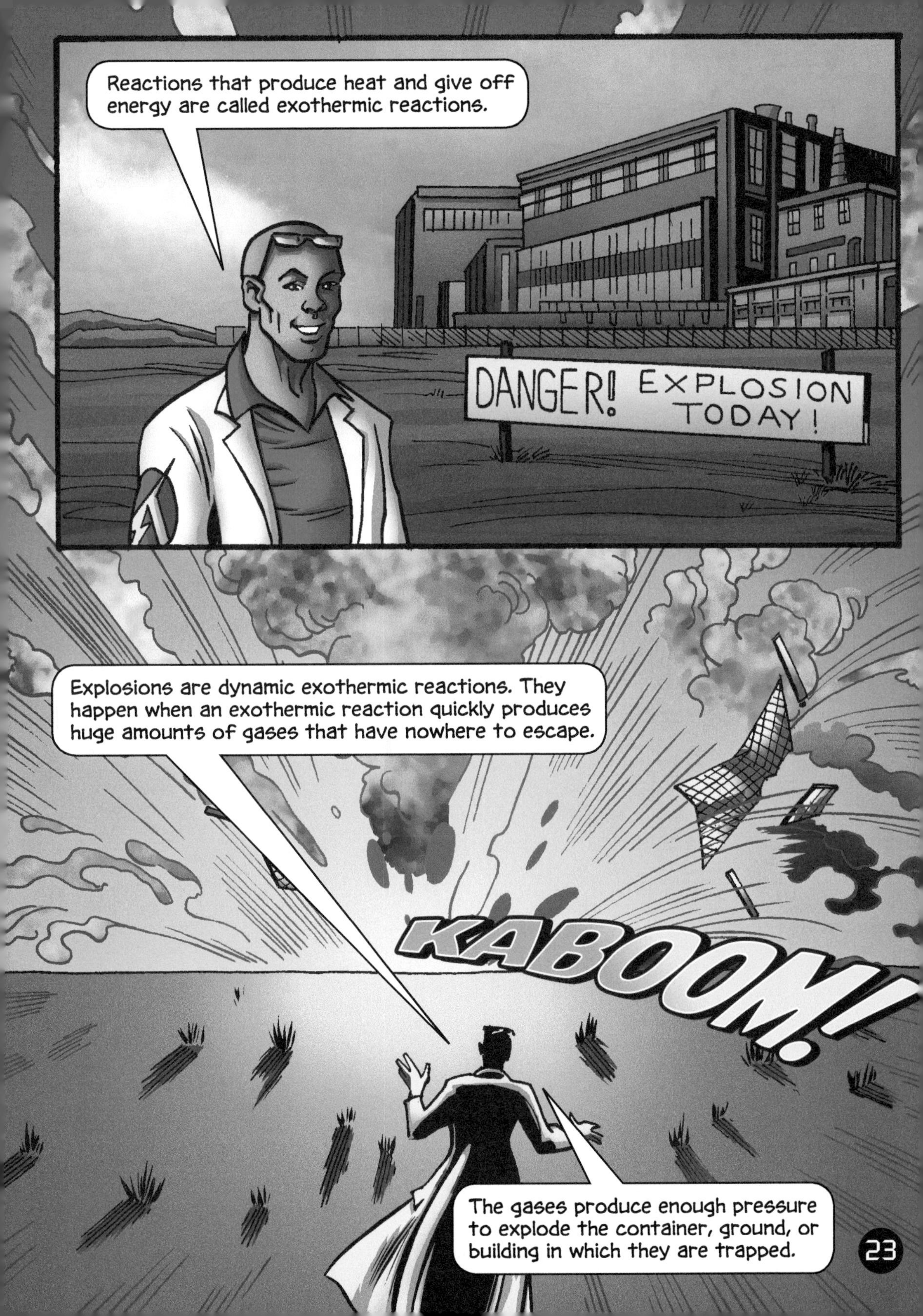

Reactions that produce heat and give off energy are called exothermic reactions.
DANGER! EXPLOSION TODAY!
Explosions are dynamic exothermic reactions. They happen when an exothermic reaction quickly produces huge amounts of gases that have nowhere to escape.
KABOOM!
The gases produce enough pressure to explode the container, ground, or building in which they are trapped.

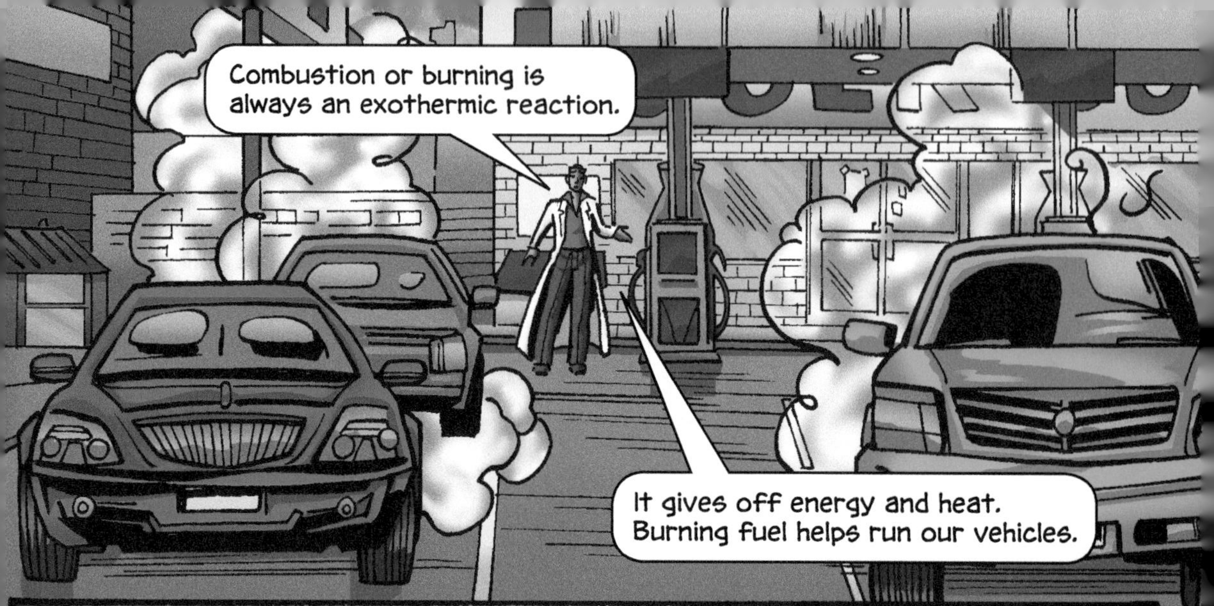
Combustion or burning is always an exothermic reaction.
It gives off energy and heat. Burning fuel helps run our vehicles.

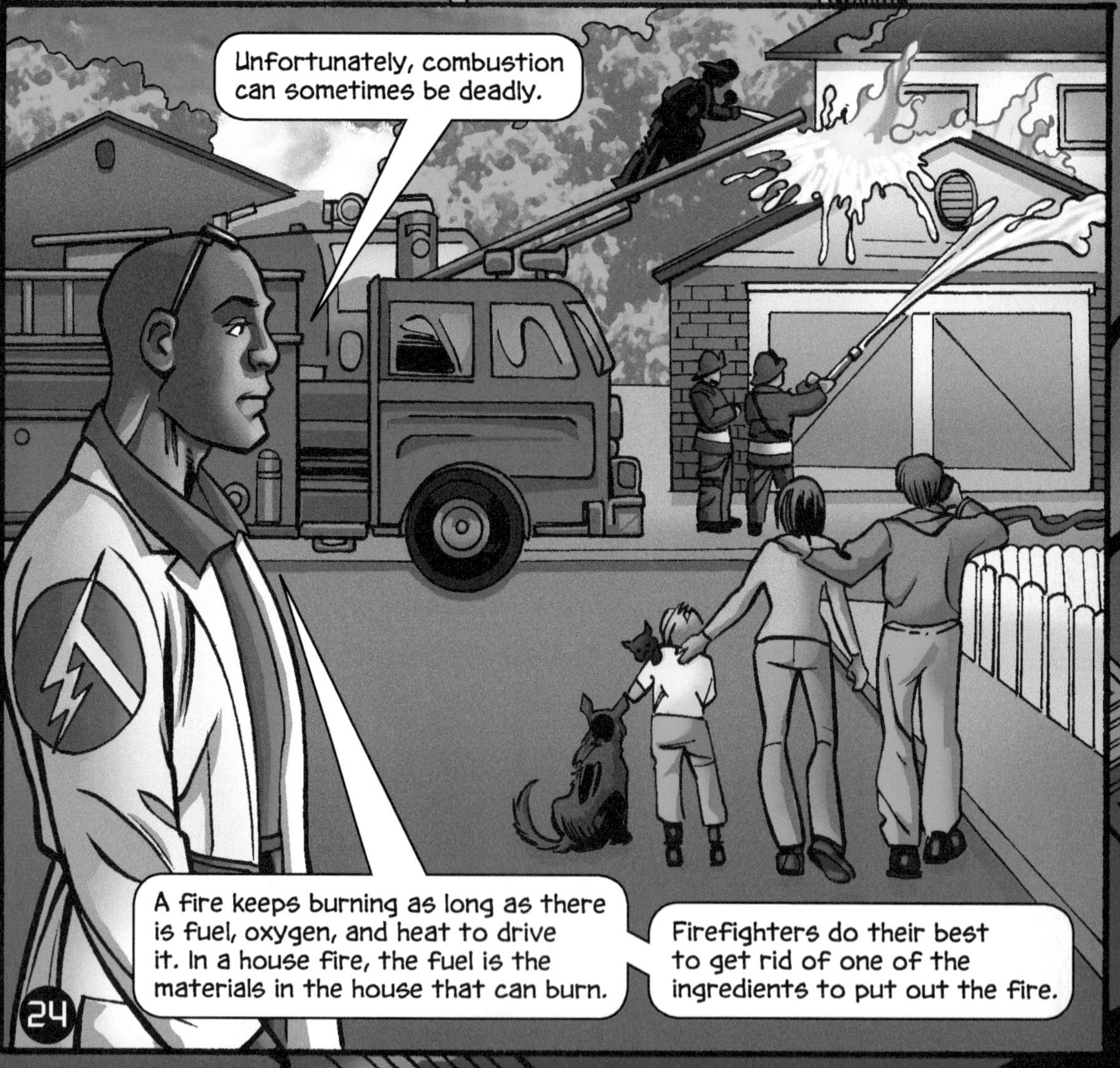
Unfortunately, combustion can sometimes be deadly.
A fire keeps burning as long as there is fuel, oxygen, and heat to drive it. In a house fire, the fuel is the materials in the house that can burn.
Firefighters do their best to get rid of one of the ingredients to put out the fire.

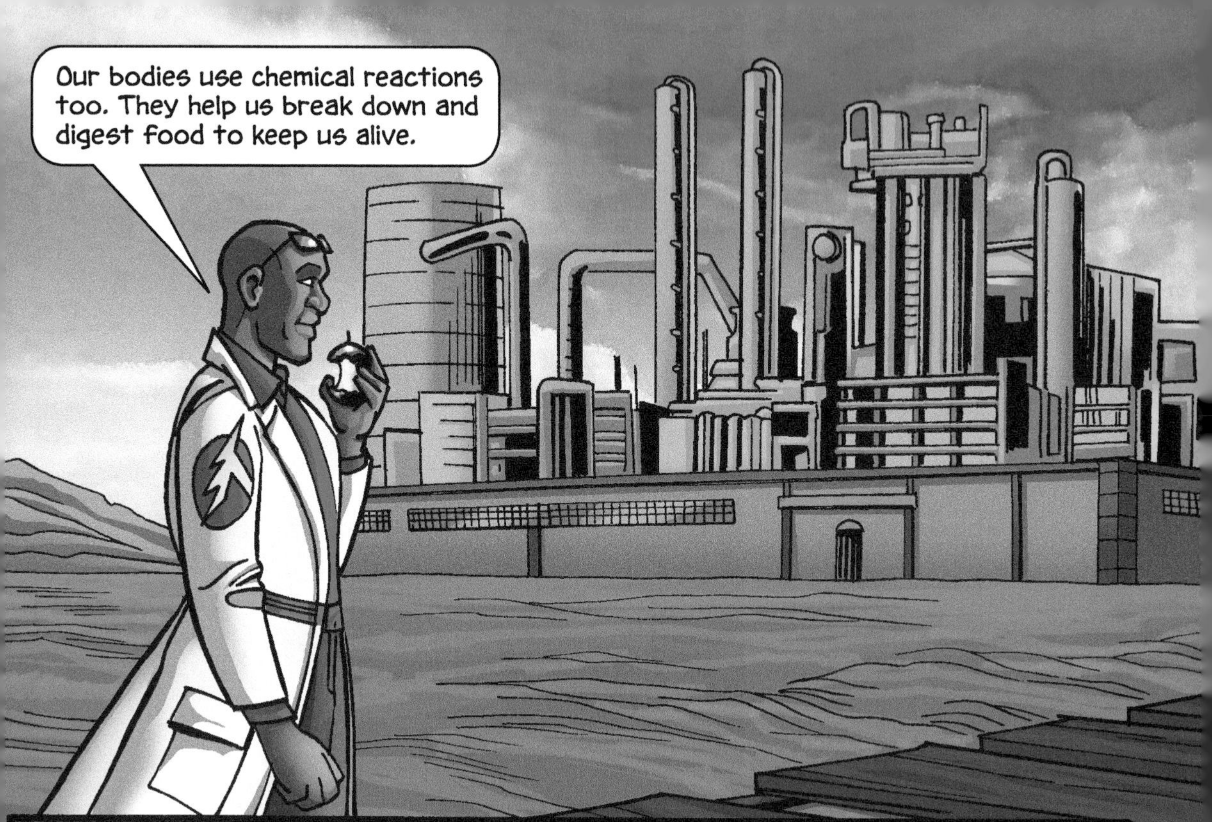
Our bodies use chemical reactions too. They help us break down and digest food to keep us alive.

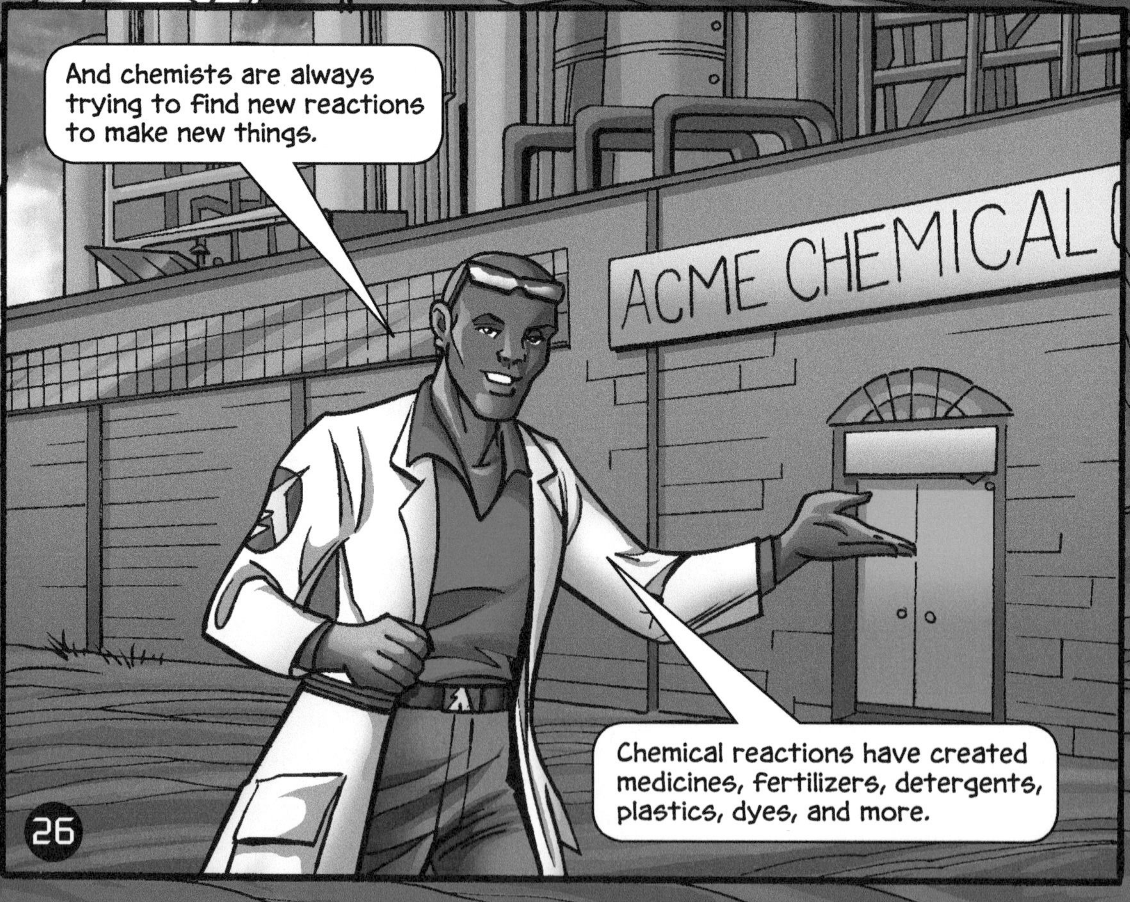
And chemists are always trying to find new reactions to make new things.
ACME CHEMICAL
Chemical reactions have created medicines, fertilizers, detergents, plastics, dyes, and more.

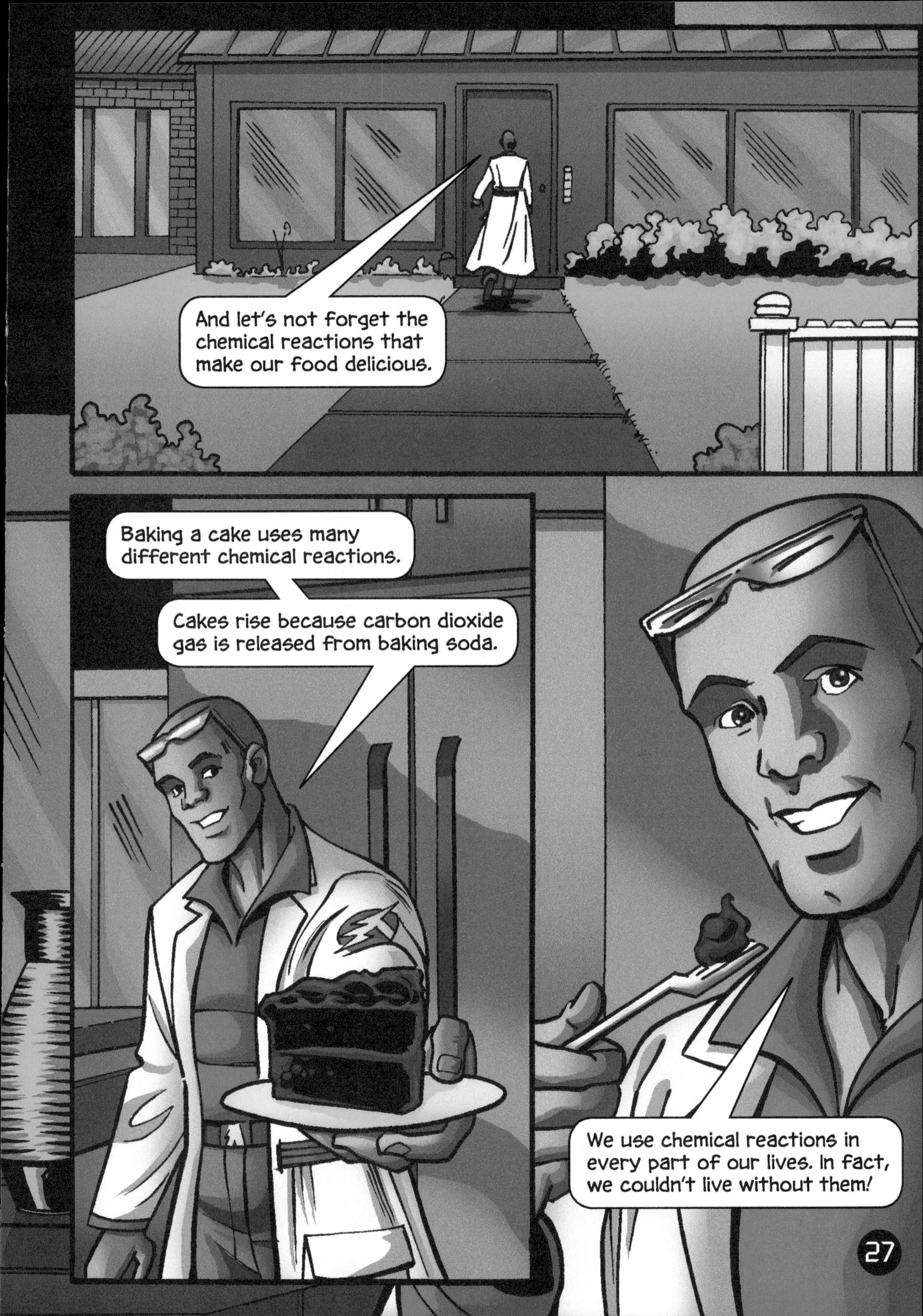
And let's not forget the chemical reactions that make our food delicious.
Baking a cake uses many different chemical reactions.
Cakes rise because carbon dioxide gas is released from baking soda.
We use chemical reactions in every part of our lives. In fact, we couldn't live without them!

CHEMICAL REACTIONS

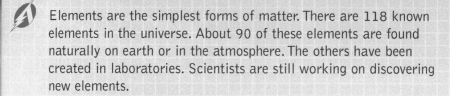

Elements are the simplest forms of matter. There are 118 known elements in the universe. About 90 of these elements are found naturally on earth or in the atmosphere. The others have been created in laboratories. Scientists are still working on discovering new elements.

A molecular formula tells you the total number and kinds of atoms in a molecule. Water's molecular formula is H_2O. That means to make a molecule of water you need two atoms of hydrogen (H) and one atom of oxygen (O). Carbon dioxide's formula is CO_2. That means you need one atom of carbon (C) and two of oxygen (O) to make a carbon dioxide molecule.

Fireflies glow because of a special reaction involving oxygen atoms and two other chemicals. The chemical reaction takes place in the firefly's abdomen. The light produced shines right through its body.

Heating chemical compounds produces the beautiful colors you see in fireworks. When heated, the compounds give off colors. To get blue, fireworks experts add copper compounds. To get orange, they add calcium.

New York's Statue of Liberty is green thanks to chemical reactions. Made of copper, the statue was originally the color of a penny. But over the years, the copper has reacted with oxygen in the air, or oxidized, to form the statue's famous green coating.

Have you ever made a volcano using baking soda and vinegar? The resulting "lava" is made by a chemical reaction. The baking soda and vinegar react to produce water, sodium acetate, and lots of fizzy carbon dioxide gas.

Acid rain is caused by sulfur dioxide and nitrogen oxides that are released into the atmosphere by human pollution or natural events. These chemicals react with water, oxygen, and other compounds to form acid rain. Acid rain has harmful effects on the environment, wildlife, and humans.

BUBBLING BLOBS

What happens when you combine oil, water, and a chemical reaction? You get a super cool lava lamp!

WHAT YOU NEED:

- 52-oz (1.5-L) plastic bottle
- vegetable oil
- pitcher of water
- food coloring
- 2 effervescent tablets

WHAT YOU DO:

1. Fill the bottle about half full with vegetable oil.

2. Slowly pour the water from the pitcher and into the bottle. Continue filling until the bottle is almost full.

3. Wait a few minutes and watch as the oil and water separate completely. Note how the water sinks to the bottom of the bottle and the oil floats on top.

4. Add about 12 drops of food coloring to the bottle.

5. Once again, wait a few minutes. Watch as the food coloring passes through the oil and mixes with the water on the bottom of the bottle.

6. Break the effervescent tablets into several pieces. Drop the tablet pieces into the bottle.

7. Watch as blobs of color begin to rise. The effervescent tablets and the water are having a chemical reaction that produces carbon dioxide gas. As the gas bubbles rise, they take some of the colored water with them. The gas escapes when it reaches the top of the bottle. Then the colored water droplets fall back down to the bottom of the bottle.

DISCUSSION QUESTIONS

1. What signs show that a chemical reaction is happening in a fire? What new substances are formed when wood burns?

2. What is the difference between a physical change and a chemical change? Give an example of each to support your answer.

3. What is the difference between an atom and a molecule? What happens to atoms and molecules during a chemical reaction?

4. Describe two chemical reactions that you have seen around your home or in nature. Why do you think those chemical reactions happened?

WRITING PROMPTS

1. Chemical reactions happen all around us. Make a list of the chemical reactions you've seen today.

2. Reread page 16. Using your own words, write a paragraph explaining how Max changes water into hydrogen peroxide. Draw pictures of the two molecules to support your explanation.

3. Imagine that you could shrink down to the size of molecules and atoms like Max. Write a short story that details which atoms and molecules you would explore and what you would do with them.

4. Exploding fireworks are examples of exothermic reactions. Think back to a time when you watched fireworks go off. Then write a paragraph describing the details you noticed about this type of chemical reaction.

GLOSSARY

atom (AT-uhm)—an element in its smallest form

combination reaction (kom-buh-NAY-shuhn ree-AK-shuhn)—a chemical reaction where two substances combine to form a new product

combustion (kuhm-BUS-chuhn)—the process of catching fire and burning

compound (KOM-pound)—something formed by combining two or more parts

decomposition reaction (dee-kom-poh-ZIH-shuhn ree-AK-shuhn)—a chemical reaction where a substance breaks down into simpler parts

electron (i-LEK-tron)—a tiny particle in an atom that travels around the nucleus

element (EL-uh-muhnt)—a basic substance in chemistry that cannot be broken down into simpler substances under ordinary lab conditions

endothermic reaction (en-doh-THUR-mic ree-AK-shuhn)—a chemical reaction that takes in energy

exothermic reaction (eks-oh-THUR-mic ree-AK-shuhn)—a chemical reaction that gives off energy

fermentation (fur-men-TAY-shuhn)—a chemical change that makes the sugar in a substance change into alcohol

matter (MAT-ur)—anything that has weight and takes up space

molecule (MOL-uh-kyool)—two or more atoms of the same or different elements that have bonded; a molecule is the smallest part of a substance that can't be divided without a chemical change

READ MORE

O'Mara, Kennon. *Atoms*. A Look at Chemistry. New York: Gareth Stevens Publishing, 2019.

Peterson, Megan Cooley. *Scooby-Doo!, A Science of Chemical Reactions Mystery: The Overreacting Ghost*. Scooby-Doo Solves it with S.T.E.M. North Mankato, Minn.: Capstone Press, 2017.

Winterberg, Jenna. *Chemical Reactions*. Huntington Beach, Calif.: Teacher Created Materials, 2016.

INTERNET SITES

Use Facthound to find Internet sites related to this book.

Visit *www.facthound.com*

Just type in 9781543558722 and go!

Check out projects, games and lots more at
www.capstonekids.com

INDEX